Bandit *cat crew* VOLUME 1

CREATED BY TOM WILSON

STORY, ART, PENCILS, INK, COLOURING AND TEXT
BY TOM WILSON.

CONTAINS ISSUES 1-4 FIRST PRINTED IN COMIC BOOK
FORMAT 2020

PRINTED IN THE UNITED KINGDOM
FIRST PRINT 2021

MERAKI COMICS
merakicomics@gmail.com

MERAKI
-COMICS-

PART 1

"THE TEMPLE OF FIRE"

ISSUE 1 · FIRST PUBLISHED 2020

AFTER SO LONG SEARCHING THE UNCHARTED JUNGLE, WE FINALLY FOUND WHAT WE CAME FOR....
I CAN'T BELIEVE IT! THE LEGEND... ALL OF IT WAS TRUE! NOW IT'S TIME TO SEE IF OUR HARD WORK IS GOING TO PAY OFF!
THE TEMPLE OF FIRE! A PLACE WHERE THEY SAY ANCIENT DIVINE POWERS CAN BE CLAIMED BY ANYONE WHO DESIRES THEM. --
BUT OF COURSE I'M JUST IN IT FOR THE RESEARCH.
WHAT DO YOU THINK? IS THIS THE PLACE OR WHAT?
LOOK AT THOSE MARKINGS... IT'S GOTTA BE!

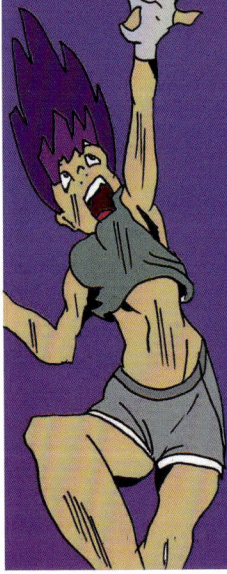

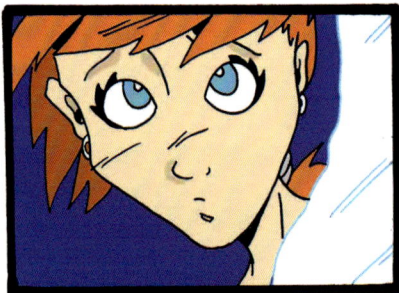

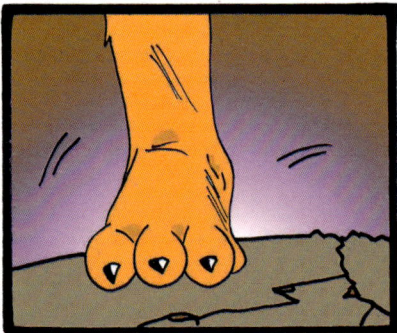

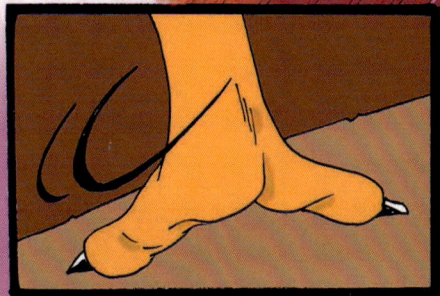

IT WAS THE LAST MEETING AT THEIR COUNCIL WHEN THEY CONTESTED MY DREAMS... MY VISION.
THEY KNOW NOTHING, THOSE ARROGANT FOOLS!
HE WHO IS CALLED VANARIS, IT IS WITH GREAT CONSIDERATION THAT THIS POWER OF YOURS, ALONG WITH THE VISION OF CONTROLLING ALL HUMAN EMPIRES IS TO BE STOPPED. I FEAR YOUR MINDSET HAS BECOME UNHINGED. IT IS THE DECISION OF THE OVERSEERS THAT YOU SHALL BE IMPRISONED FOR YOUR CRIMES.
TAKE THIS HERETIC AWAY.
HOW DARE YOU!!
YOU CAN'T DO THIS TO ME! YOU'RE NOTHING BUT A COWARD! WHEN I GET OUT YOU'RE ALL FINISHED!!

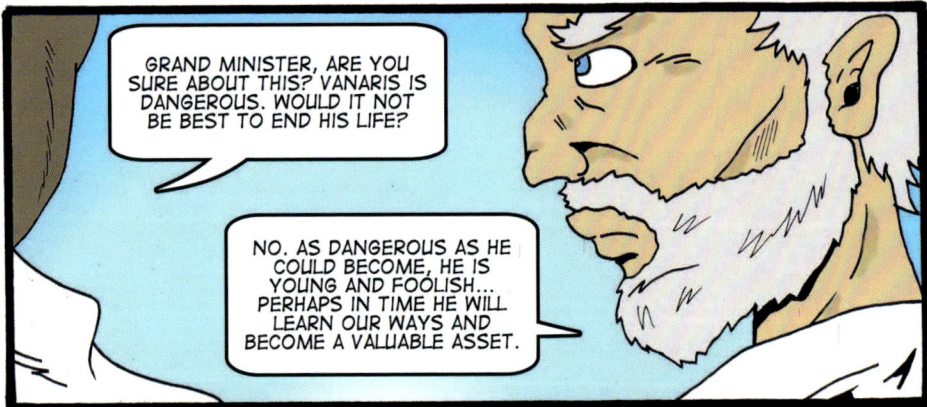

AWWW YEAH!! BANDIT CAT HEADQUARTERS BABY!!
HEY BUSTER LET'S GET ONE THING STRAIGHT! IT'S MY HOME - NOT SOME SUPER HERO HANGOUT!!
DETAILS, DETAILS! NOW GO FORTH! TO THE FORTRESS OF SADIE!
GGRRR! YOU'RE WALKING OR THE DEALS OFF!

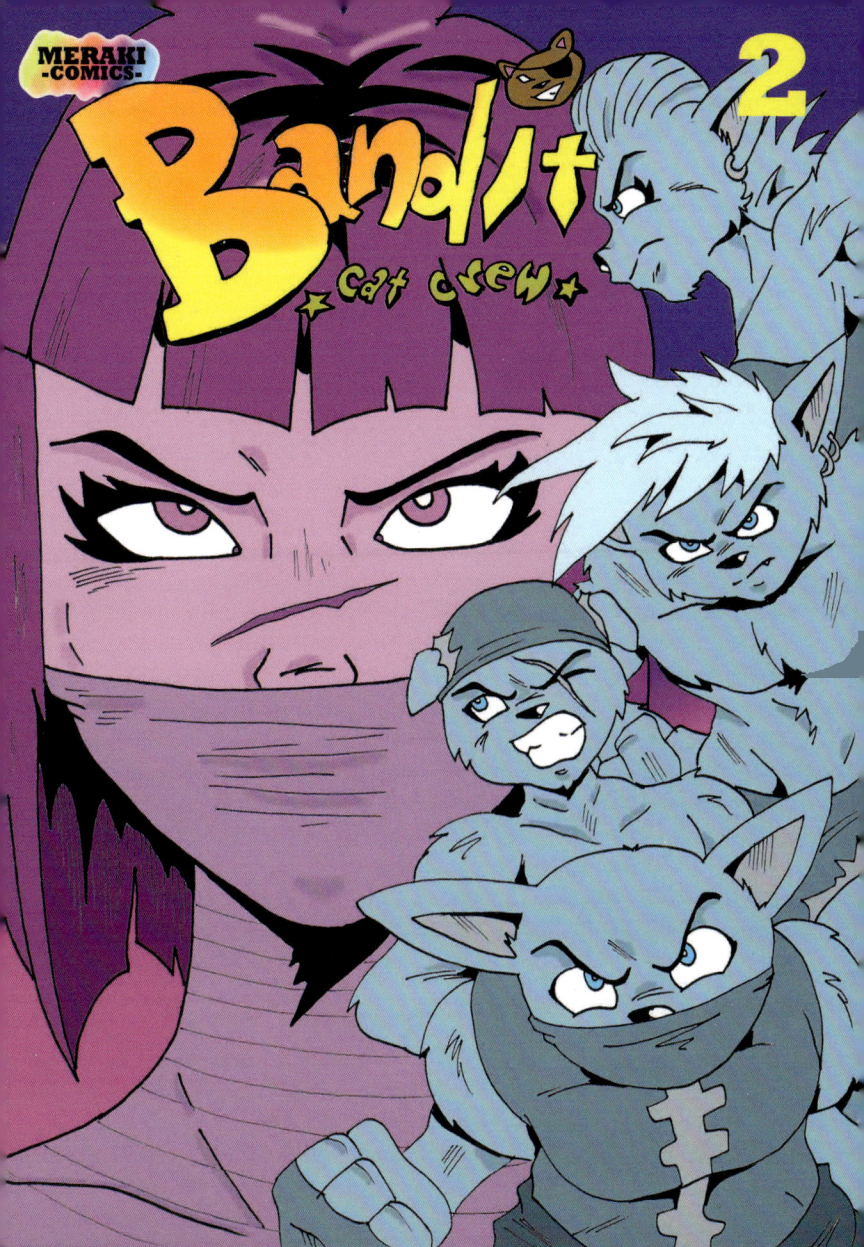

AFTER ESCAPING THE TEMPLE OF FIRE OUR HEROES FIND THEMSELVES IN THE CLEARING.

WE'VE MADE IT, OUT OF THE JUNGLE AND INTO THE DESERT.

MORE LIKE OUT OF THE FRYING PAN AND INTO THE FIRE.

QUIT YOUR MOANING ZIEK, WE'RE OUT OF THAT TOMB. WHO CARES IF IT'S HOT.

LET'S JUST GET TO SADIE'S HOME SO WE CAN FIGURE OUT WHAT'S GOING ON.

IN-INCREDIBLE, THESE CREATURES... THEY.. THEY CAME FROM THE GODS?
IF WE CAN HARNESS THEIR POWER....
YOUR MISSION IS TO RETRIEVE THE SUBJECTS. DO NOT FAIL!
AS YOU COMMAND, BUT THIS ISN'T AN ARTIFACT.. MY PRICE HAS JUST TRIPLED!
MONEY IS OF NO CONCERN. BRING THEM BACK ALIVE... THEN WE WILL DISCUSS YOUR PAYMENT.
KEEP YOUR GOONS AWAY. I HAVE A... SPECIAL TASK FORCE TO HANDLE THIS!

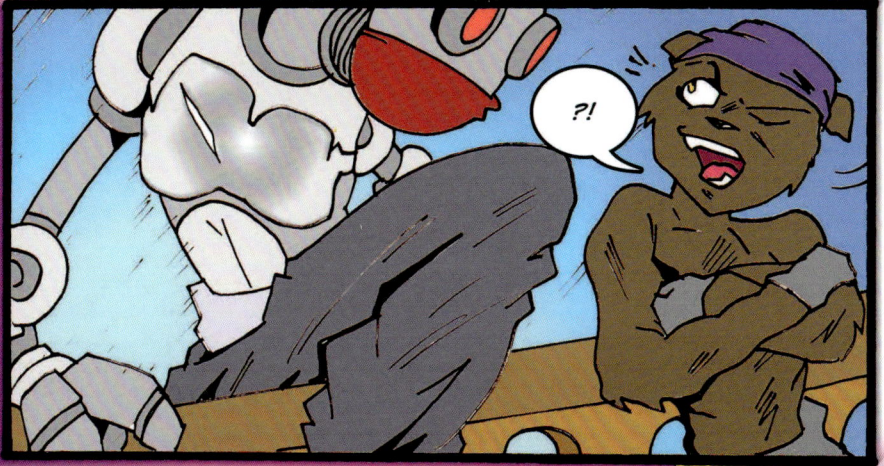

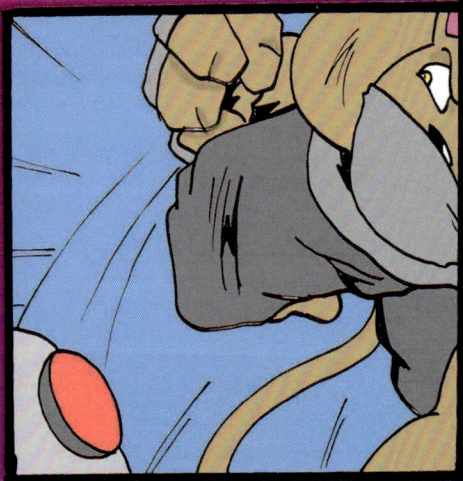

WHAT'S WRONG? MAYBE YOUR BATTERY IS DUD!

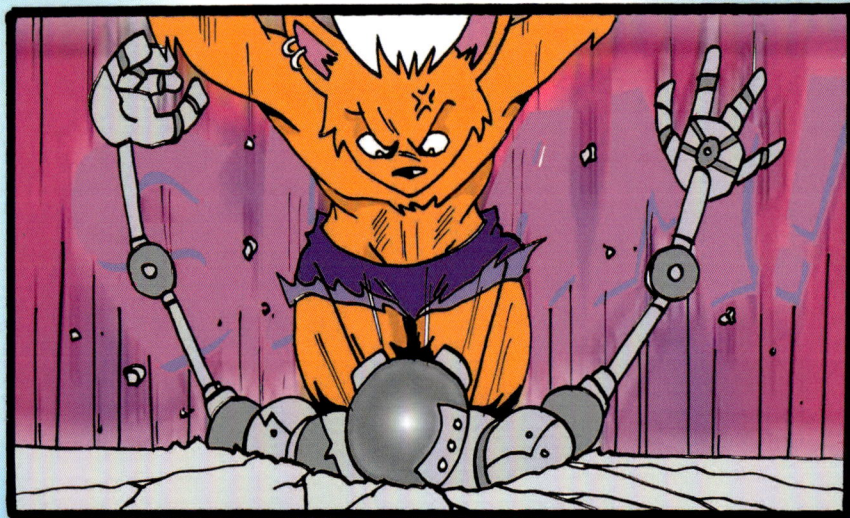

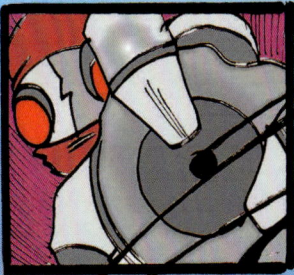

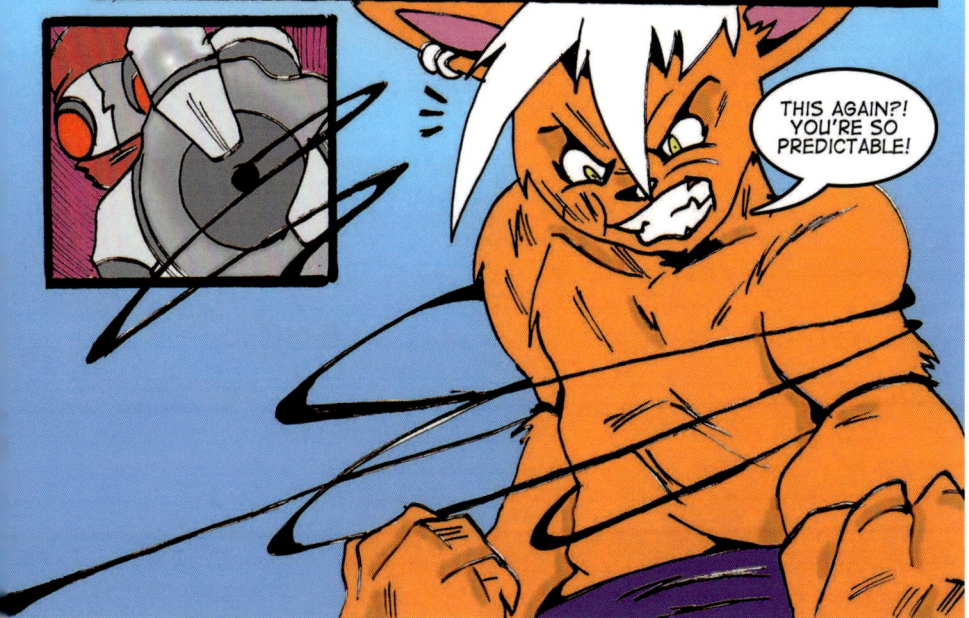

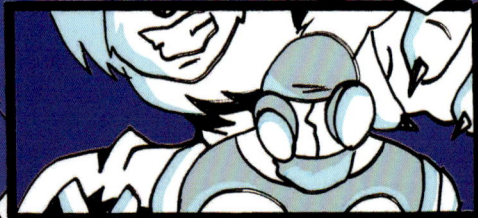

"ENTER THE COORDINATES SO WE CAN ENGAGE AUTO PILOT TO REACH THE BASE."
WAKE UP!
YOUR FRIENDS MAY HAVE ESCAPED BUT YOU BELONG TO ME NOW! AND I'M GOING TO SELL YOU TO A VERY INTERESTED BUYER!
YOU MONSTER! WHEN THEY FIND ME THEY'LL TEAR YOU AND YOUR TOYS APART!

I COULD FEEL IT... I KNEW SOMETHING WAS UP. HOW COULD WE HAVE LET THIS HAPPEN.
HEY C'MON GUYS DON'T SWEAT IT! WE GOT THE TRACKER, WE KNOW EXACTLY WHERE TO GO!
YEAH! THEY WONT BE EXPECTING THAT, YOU KNOW.. IT MIGHT JUST GIVE US AN EDGE!
ZIEK I WANT YOU AND MUKK TO HANDLE THIS.

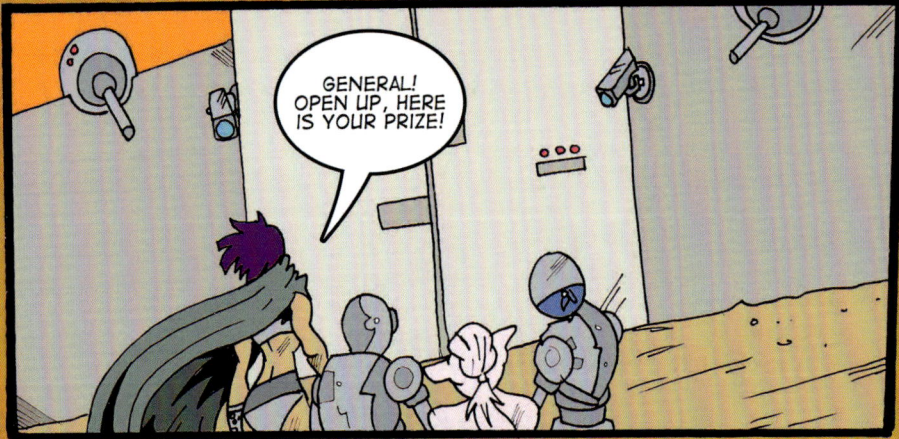

PART 3
"THE GREAT ESCAPE"

FIRST PUBLISHED 2021

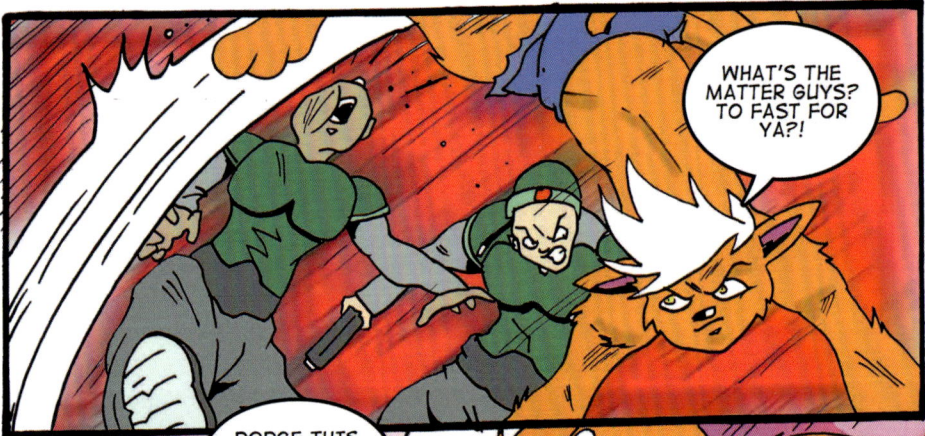

BUT OF COURSE SHE KNOWS ME, WE ENTERED THE TEMPLE TOGETHER!

LUCIA! YOUR ALIVE! B-BUT I THOUGHT YOU DIED!

I'M SO SORRY I TRIED TO GET TO YOU IN TIME BUT YOU WERE JUST OUT OF REACH...

I WATCHED YOU FALL INTO DARKNESS... AND I COULDN'T HEAR YOUR VOICE I THOUGHT YOU WERE DEAD.

IF I'D HAD KNOWN I WOULD HAVE FOUND A WAY TO FIND YOU. PLEASE FORGIVE ME.

** SEE ISSUE NUMBER 1

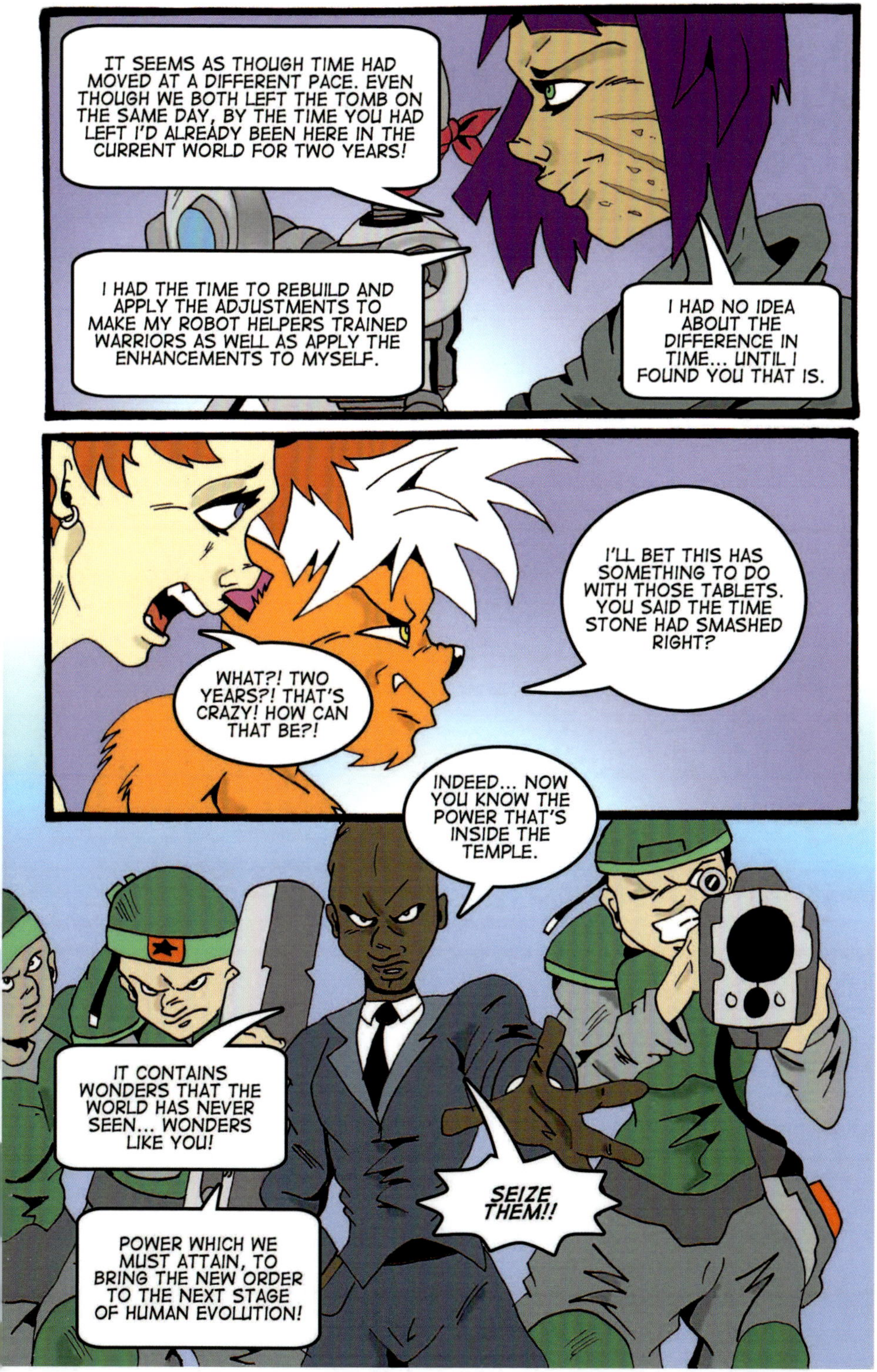
IT SEEMS AS THOUGH TIME HAD MOVED AT A DIFFERENT PACE. EVEN THOUGH WE BOTH LEFT THE TOMB ON THE SAME DAY, BY THE TIME YOU HAD LEFT I'D ALREADY BEEN HERE IN THE CURRENT WORLD FOR TWO YEARS!
I HAD THE TIME TO REBUILD AND APPLY THE ADJUSTMENTS TO MAKE MY ROBOT HELPERS TRAINED WARRIORS AS WELL AS APPLY THE ENHANCEMENTS TO MYSELF.
I HAD NO IDEA ABOUT THE DIFFERENCE IN TIME... UNTIL I FOUND YOU THAT IS.
WHAT?! TWO YEARS?! THAT'S CRAZY! HOW CAN THAT BE?!
I'LL BET THIS HAS SOMETHING TO DO WITH THOSE TABLETS. YOU SAID THE TIME STONE HAD SMASHED RIGHT?
INDEED... NOW YOU KNOW THE POWER THAT'S INSIDE THE TEMPLE.
IT CONTAINS WONDERS THAT THE WORLD HAS NEVER SEEN... WONDERS LIKE YOU!
POWER WHICH WE MUST ATTAIN, TO BRING THE NEW ORDER TO THE NEXT STAGE OF HUMAN EVOLUTION!
SEIZE THEM!!

YOU AND YOUR MEN STAY OUT OF THIS! I WILL CAPTURE THESE CREATURES!
KINDA WISHING VETT WAS HERE RIGHT NOW.
WE'RE BOTH STRONGER BUT WE'RE OUTNUMBERED BIG TIME!
EEEEK! WHAT ARE WE GOING TO DO WE CAN'T FIGHT THEM ALL CAN WE?!
IT'S EITHER THAT OR END UP IN CAGES!

MEANWHILE......
"SIGH"
I'M SO BORED, WHY DOES DAD BRING ME HERE JUST TO SIT IN A ROOM?!
FORGET THIS! I'M GOING EXPLORING. THERE'S GOTTA BE SOMETHING TO DO AROUND HERE!
WHOA...
WAAA! WHOOPS I DIDN'T MEAN TO OPEN THE DOOR!

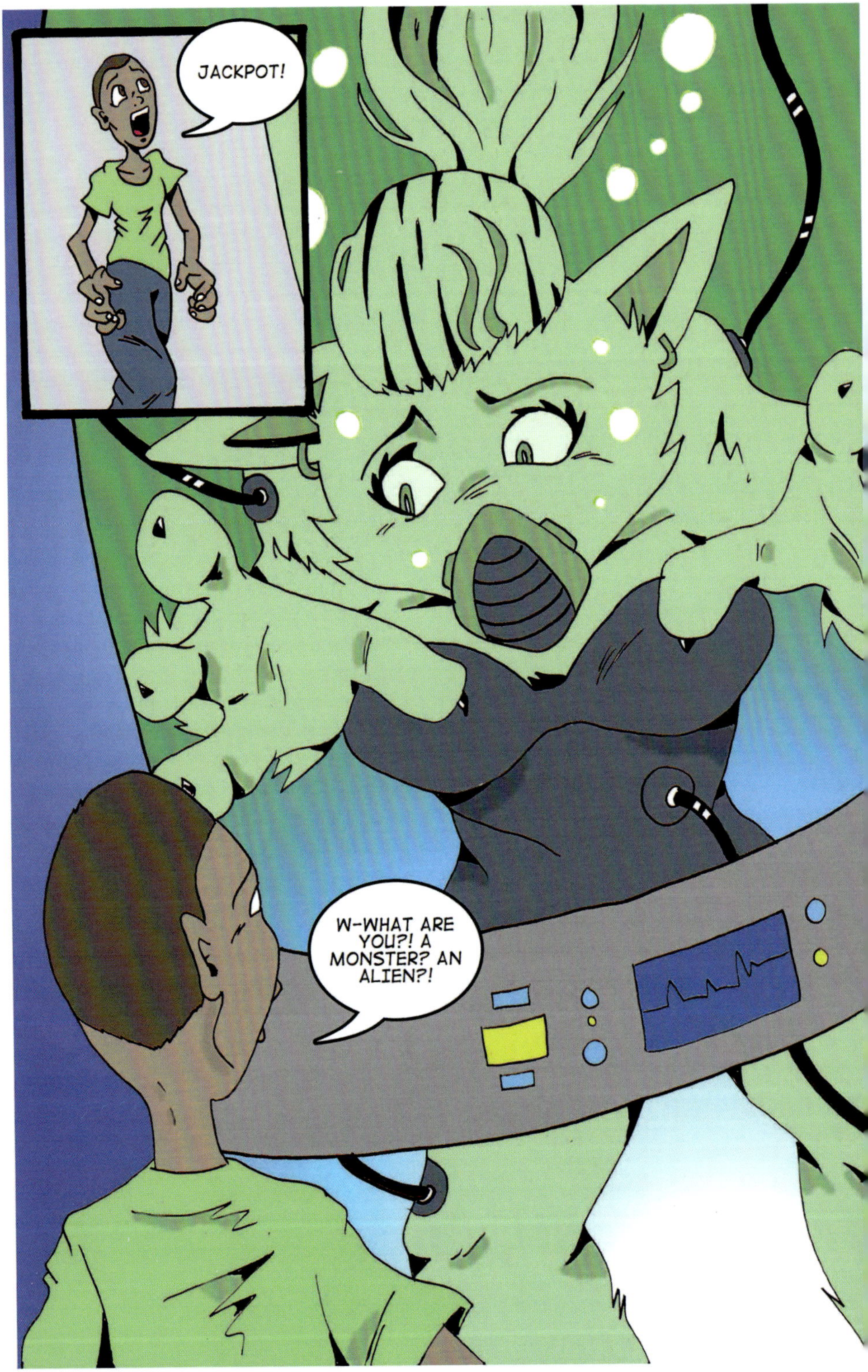
JACKPOT!
W-WHAT ARE YOU?! A MONSTER? AN ALIEN?!

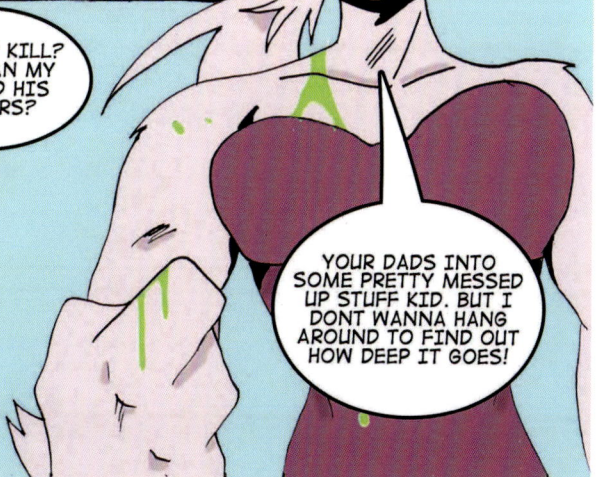

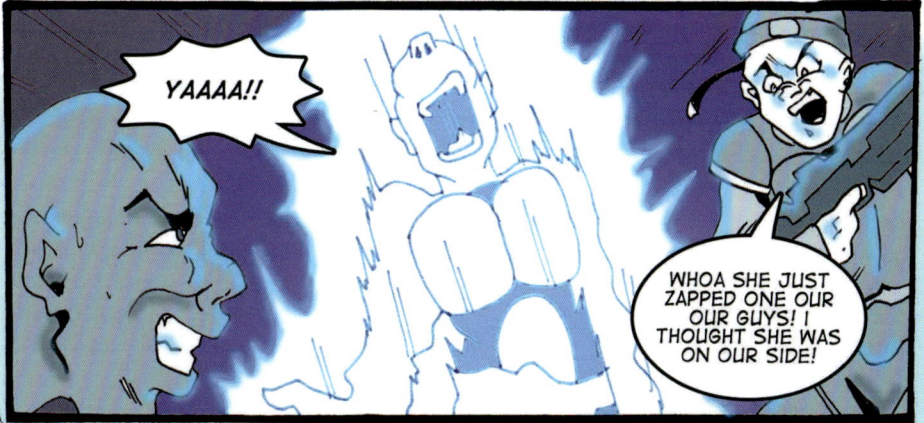

PART 4
"DEMONS ON THE HILL"

FIRST PUBLISHED 2021

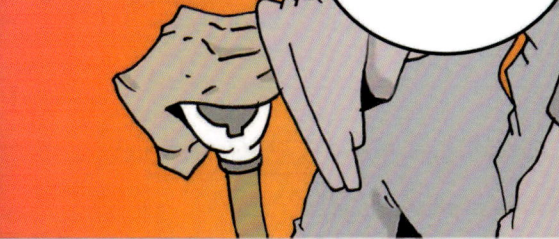

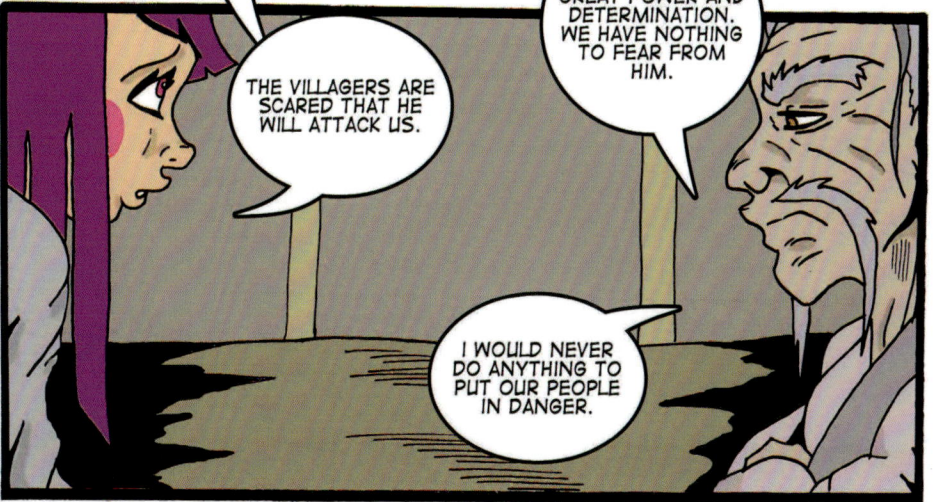

HMM PERHAPS YOU AREN'T INVOLVED AFTER ALL. IN REGARDS TO US HUMANS, WE ARE RIVAL VILLAGERS. I COME FROM THE EAST WHILST CURRENTLY WE ARE IN THE NORTH. I WAS CAPTURED...
BUT WE WERE NOT FIGHTING THE VILLAGERS, WE WERE FIGHTING THE MONSTER.... THE OTHER ONE LIKE YOU.
WHAT?! BUT THAT CAN'T BE. MY SIBLINGS AND I ARE THE ONLY ONES OF OUR KIND LEFT!
I HAVE SEEN HIM WITH MY OWN EYES.... AND I AM THE ONLY ONE WHO SURVIVED.
IT WAS A FEW DAYS AGO.
OKAY MEN, THAT WIZARD IS IN THIS TEMPLE. HIS DARK MAGIC IS FORBIDDEN AND HE MUST BE STOPPED.

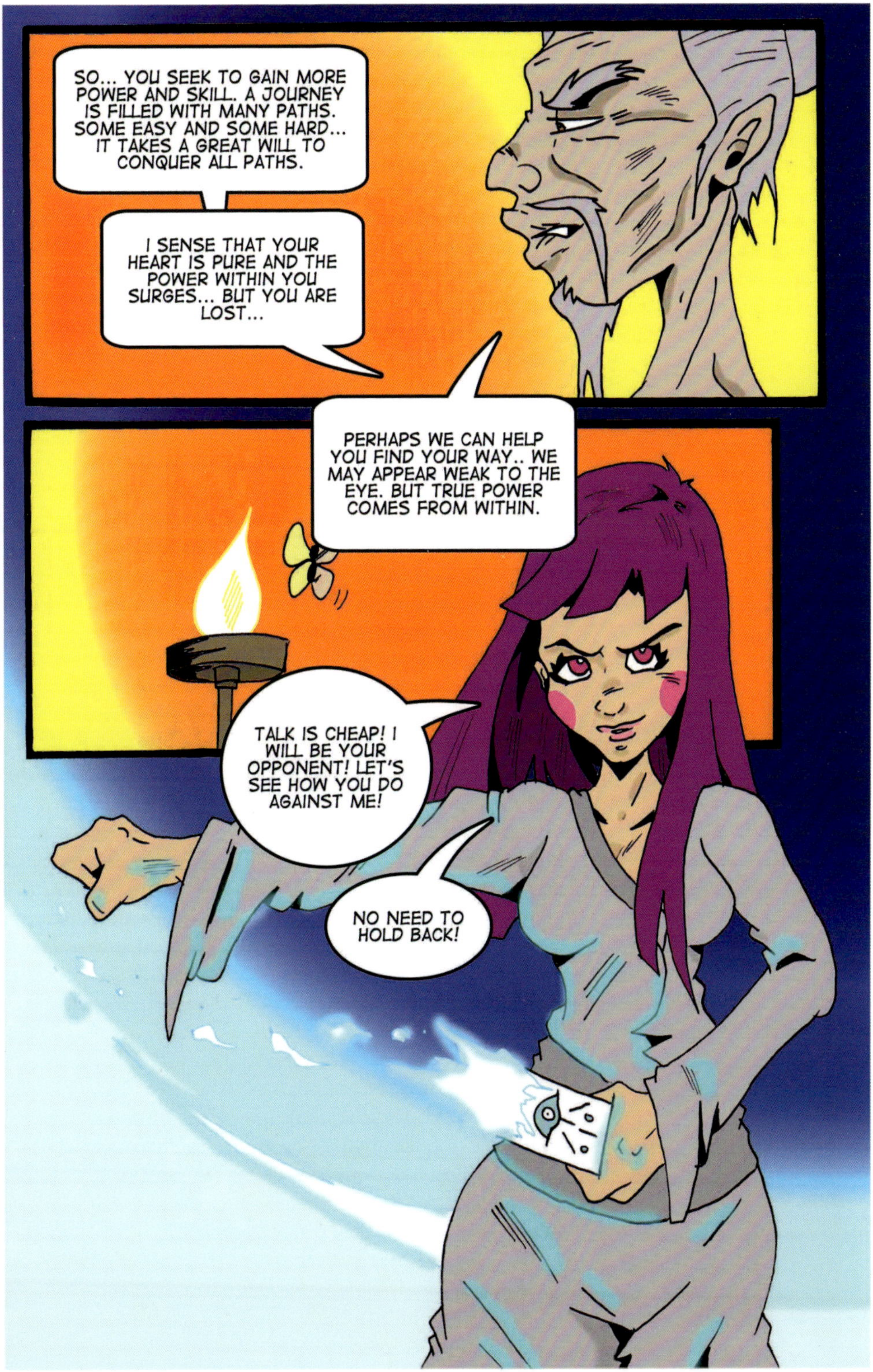
SO... YOU SEEK TO GAIN MORE POWER AND SKILL. A JOURNEY IS FILLED WITH MANY PATHS. SOME EASY AND SOME HARD... IT TAKES A GREAT WILL TO CONQUER ALL PATHS.
I SENSE THAT YOUR HEART IS PURE AND THE POWER WITHIN YOU SURGES... BUT YOU ARE LOST...
PERHAPS WE CAN HELP YOU FIND YOUR WAY.. WE MAY APPEAR WEAK TO THE EYE. BUT TRUE POWER COMES FROM WITHIN.
TALK IS CHEAP! I WILL BE YOUR OPPONENT! LET'S SEE HOW YOU DO AGAINST ME!
NO NEED TO HOLD BACK!

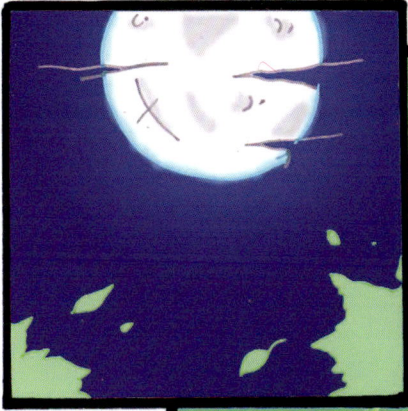

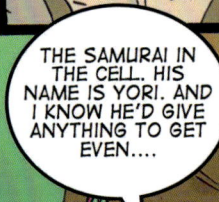

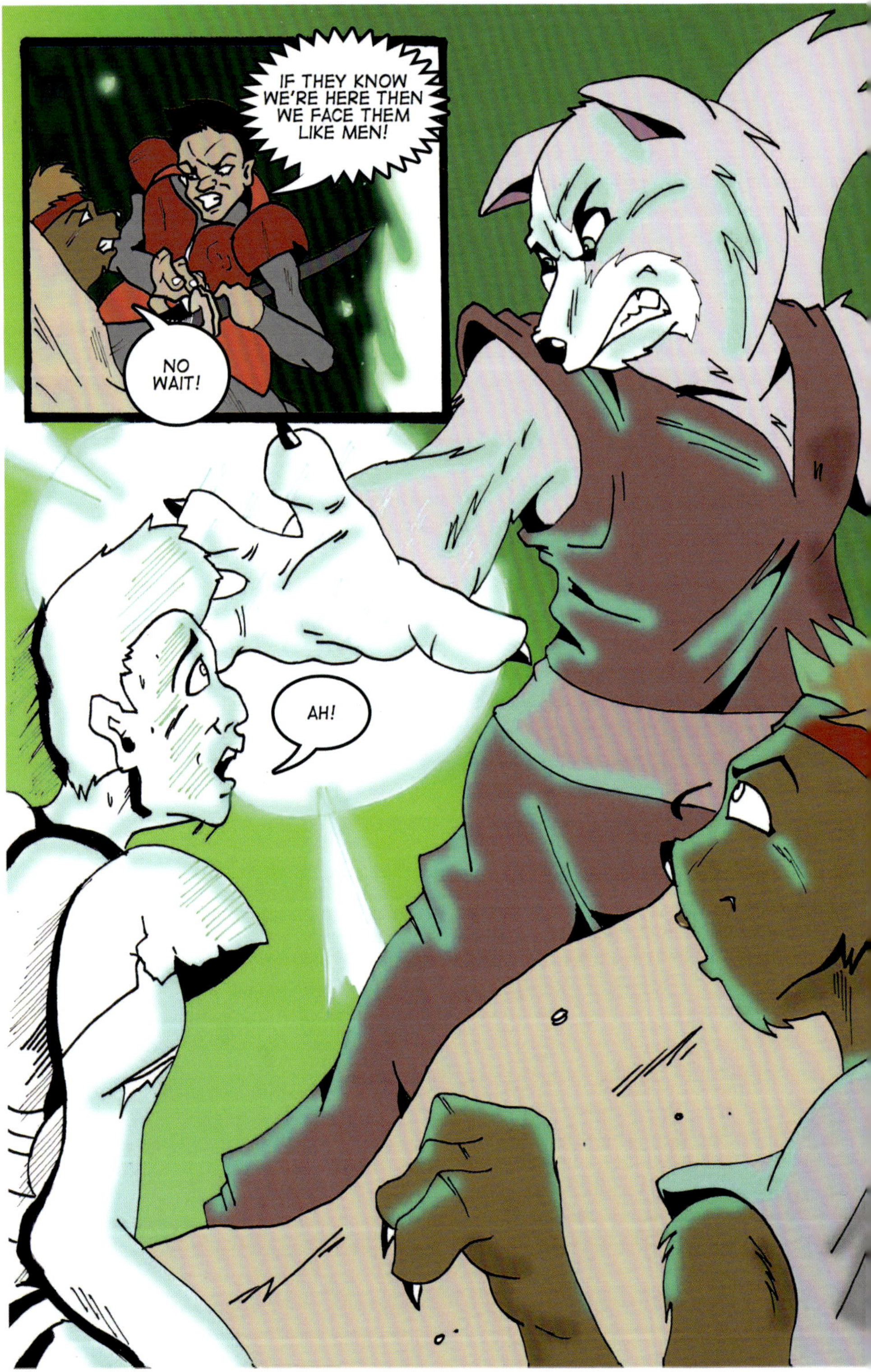
IF THEY KNOW WE'RE HERE THEN WE FACE THEM LIKE MEN!
NO WAIT!
AH!

Hello Everyone!
(A note from the Author)

I would like to take a quick moment to thank everyone who
has purchased and supported this book. I would like to thank
the readers and the retailers that supply my titles. It
is because of you and your support that i am able to do what I do
and that this dream has become a reality.
I can not express how greatful I am and I can't wait to meet
all the fans of the series at comic cons and events.
Bandit Cat Crew - Book 2 featuring issues (5-8) will be on
the way as well as other titles in the near future.
Please follow us on Facebook and instagram for the latest updates
and infomation regarding Meraki titles and events.

I hope you enjoyed the book.

Thank you,

Tom Wilson
Meraki Comics

MERAKI
-COMICS-